STAND AGAINST

POVERTY AND HUNGER

Alice Harman

PowerKiDS press
New York

Published in 2023 by The Rosen Publishing Group, Inc.
29 East 21st Street, New York, NY 10010

Copyright © 2023 Franklin Watts, a division of Hachette Children's Group

All rights reserved. No part of this book may be reproduced in any form without permission in writing from the publisher, except by a reviewer.

Designer and illustrator: Mimi Butler

Cataloging-in-Publication Data

Names: Harman, Alice.
Title: Poverty and hunger / Alice Harman.
Description: New York : PowerKids Press, 2023. | Series: Stand against | Includes glossary and index.
Identifiers: ISBN 9781725339002 (pbk.) | ISBN 9781725339019 (library bound) | ISBN 9781725339026 (ebook)
Subjects: LCSH: Poverty--Juvenile literature. | Hunger--Juvenile literature. | Poverty--Prevention--Juvenile literature.
Classification: LCC HC79.P6 H355 2023 | DDC 362.5'8--dc23

Manufactured in the United States of America

Find us on 	 Batch #CSPK23. For further information contact Rosen Publishing, New York, New York at 1-800-237-9932.

CONTENTS

POVERTY AND HUNGER TODAY — 4
CHECK YOUR CONSUMPTION — 6
FOOD AVAILABILITY — 8
FOOD DISTRIBUTION — 10
FOOD QUALITY — 12
STAND AGAINST: FOOD INEQUALITY — 14
CLIMATE CHANGE — 16
INTENSIVE FARMING — 18
PESTICIDES AND HERBICIDES — 20
GROWING TECHNOLOGIES — 22
STAND AGAINST: FOOD DESTRUCTION — 24
NO WAY TO WORK — 26
IN-WORK POVERTY — 28
MODERN SLAVERY — 30
STAND AGAINST: CHILD LABOR — 32
HOUSING — 34
WELFARE SYSTEMS — 36
THE POWER OF PRIVILEGE — 38
STAYING AFLOAT — 40
STAND AGAINST: CHILD POVERTY — 42
BE THE CHANGE, SPREAD THE WORD — 44
GLOSSARY — 46
FURTHER INFORMATION — 47
INDEX — 48

POVERTY AND HUNGER TODAY

In the simplest terms, poverty means not having much money and hunger means not having much food. But the world is much more complicated than this, and poverty can look very different in richer countries and poorer ones.

A DEADLY PROBLEM

Every day, thousands of people die due to hunger. Many more suffer and develop serious health problems because they don't have enough food or can only afford unhealthy food.

Hunger isn't the only way poverty can be dangerous and even deadly, either. People may not have clean water to drink, a safe place to live or proper healthcare when they are ill or injured, and they could be forced to risk their lives working in terrible conditions.

THINK AND ACT

When we see statistics about people suffering and dying, it can be hard to relate to them as individuals. Imagine a child your own age, who is really scared they're going to starve to death. Write them a pledge letter, promising you'll do whatever you can to help them.

POVERTY AMONG RICHES

Not everyone suffering due to poverty and hunger is at immediate risk of dying from it. In richer countries, some people in poverty may live in better conditions generally than many people in poorer countries. However, that doesn't stop them from going hungry or having an unfairly low quality of life compared to those around them.

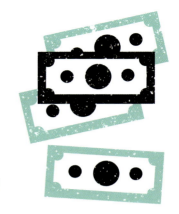

AN UNFAIR SYSTEM

There is no need for anyone to go hungry or suffer in poverty – we have more than enough money and food in the world to go around. Poverty and hunger exist because of inequality – that is, some people taking too much and leaving too little for others – and because of people's unwillingness to make things fair.

Much of our world is set up in a way that makes it easy for the rich to get richer, and extremely hard for people in poverty – and their children – to ever escape it, without changes happening on a large scale.

Read on for more information about poverty and hunger, and how to stand against them!

CHECK YOUR CONSUMPTION

The majority of people in the world don't have enough money to buy anything more than the essentials they need to survive. But many people in richer countries, and very rich people in poorer countries, often buy and use far more than they need. We call this overconsumption, and it's not just unfair – it can have a direct impact on those already struggling to survive and meet their basic needs.

BUY, BUY, BUY

How many ads do you think you've seen today – whether online, on TV, or on billboards in the street? Companies spend huge amounts of money trying to convince us to buy new things, often by making us feel like we'll miss out or won't fit in if we don't have them.

If we have enough money to buy them, it's usually not long until we're made to feel we need something new and different – so the cycle of over-consumption never stops. People can get deeply into debt trying to keep up, and it can be very difficult to pay back the money.

WASTE, WASTE, WASTE

What happens to all of these shiny new things once we don't want them any more? Usually, they go in the trash. But the issue isn't just that the thrownaway items and packaging going into a landfill — it's all the precious energy and resources wasted creating and transporting them.

Constantly racing through this "buy it and toss it" cycle at such high speed is destroying our environment and causing climate change. And the most unfair part? The world's poorest people are likely to be the worst affected by climate change, despite doing the least to cause it.

For one week, make a note every time you want to buy something — whether or not you actually buy it. Ask yourself: Do I really need it? What's making me want to buy it?

At the end of the week, look back over all your notes. How many of these things do you still care about buying, now that the moment has passed? Try a no-buy week, where you only spend money on experiences — not more stuff.

FOOD AVAILABILITY

There are around 7.7 billion people on Earth, and every year we grow enough food to feed ten billion people. Yet there are still a billion people in the world who regularly can't afford to buy enough food.

FOR RICHER, NOT POORER

Most people in richer countries, and the richest people in poorer countries, consume many times more resources than the world's poorer majority. Companies try to make more money by devoting lots of land and crops to these rich customers rather than growing cheap food for poorer people.

Many of the world's poorest people are trying to survive on farms too small to properly feed themselves. They go hungry because they can't afford to buy any extra food.

ANIMALS EAT, PEOPLE DON'T

Another issue is that a lot of crops are grown to feed animals rather than people. Animal products are too expensive for many to buy – most vegetarians in the world don't eat meat because they can't afford it, not out of choice.

Raising animals for meat and other products uses more natural resources than growing plants for people to eat directly. Companies buy up huge areas of land around the world to graze animals, sometimes forcing local indigenous people off their land.

THINK AND ACT

You don't have to be fully vegetarian or vegan for it to make a real difference in the amount of resources your dinner is using up. Try one meat-free day a week – Meatless Monday is a big campaign with a hashtag on social media where you can find lots of recipe ideas.

ENERGY OVER FOOD

Burning fossil fuels, such as coal and gas, pumps out gases that cause climate change – so surely any alternative, less polluting way to get energy is a good thing, right? But some people aren't so sure about biofuel, which is made mostly from living plants. They believe that feeding people has to come first, and worry about how much potential food-growing space is taken up growing cheap crops to produce biofuel.

There are similar worries about covering fields with solar panels, so this land produces energy rather than food.

FOOD DISTRIBUTION

Food often travels thousands of miles across the world to end up on a supermarket shelf in a rich country. But sometimes people go hungry even when food is available and they have money to buy it, because although the food is relatively close by they can't actually reach it.

ROAD TRANSPORTATION

In poorer countries, there often aren't as many roads, and they may be in such poor condition that it's almost impossible to move food from one area to another. This is even more of a problem in bad weather or after natural disasters.

People in rural areas of these countries are often at the highest risk of starvation, and if their own crops fail it is very dangerous if food can't reach them by road. Climate change is linked to an increased risk of unpredictable weather and crop failure, so this problem is likely to get worse.

CONFLICT AND CRIME

War, conflict, and crime can make areas too dangerous to travel to or through, making it difficult for food to reach the people there. Farmers may also have their food taken by fighters or criminals, and not be able to buy more. Drones are being used more and more to carry food packages, as — unlike with emergency food drops from helicopters — there are no humans on board to get hurt if they are shot down.

FOOD DESERTS

Food distribution isn't just an issue in poorer countries and conflict zones, though. In some areas of rich countries, such Atlanta and New York City in the United States, it is very difficult for people to buy fresh, unprocessed food in their local area.

These areas are called food deserts. People living there who can't afford a car or public transportation can only really buy unhealthy, heavily processed food. This food inequality is linked to serious health problems, such as heart disease.

THINK AND ACT

Emergency relief charities such as the **Red Cross** transport food and other lifesaving supplies to people affected by conflict and natural disasters.

How could you raise money to support their work? Think of some fun ideas – and encourage others to join you and help fundraise, too!

FOOD QUALITY

Everyone who goes hungry is malnourished, meaning that their body isn't getting enough nutrients. Many more people have diets with enough calories for basic survival, but not much nutritional value. This can have serious health consequences — particularly for children.

UNBALANCED DIET

Many people in poverty have to eat so cheaply that they can't afford the balanced, nutritious diet that their body needs to stay healthy.

People in extreme rural poverty, usually in poorer countries, often only eat the very limited types of food that they can grow themselves. People in these countries who live in urban poverty, without land to grow any food, rely on the cheapest, most filling foods available — such as rice, grains, bread, and starchy vegetables.

HIDDEN HUNGER

"Hidden hunger" is when people have enough food to eat but the quality is so poor that their health still suffers. Many people in richer countries now suffer from malnutrition and obesity at the same time.

People in poverty understandably try to avoid hunger by buying high-calorie, filling foods, but these often have little nutritional value. Food bank users also depend on whatever food is available, which may not include much fresh, healthy food.

HOME COOKING

Although it can be cheaper and healthier to cook certain fresh meals from scratch, especially those that don't include meat, it can also take longer – and require more regular shopping trips, as fresh foods may go bad more quickly than processed ones.

People working too many hours for too little money often don't have the time or energy to do all this, especially if they have children or health issues. Many people don't have the space or cooking facilities to easily store and prepare food, and people with certain disabilities may face additional challenges when it comes to home cooking.

THINK AND ACT

Research shows that people in poverty know which foods are healthy but they simply can't afford to buy them. Governments can subsidize healthy foods – pay money to make them cheaper to buy. Find out who your state and local officials are and write to them about this issue. Start a petition or put on an event to show how many local people care!

STAND AGAINST: FOOD INEQUALITY

Emergency solutions to hunger and malnutrition — such as food banks and helicopter food drops — give short-term help to people in desperate situations. But they are expensive to run and don't tackle the underlying causes of poverty. To stand against food inequality, we also need to think about creating long-term change.

BIG-PICTURE THINKING

Short-term solutions can be like putting a bandage on a deep cut that needs stitches — it doesn't actually solve the problem. It's important to think about why things are the way they are and how we can change them for good.

ACTIVITY

Run a donation drive for a local food bank, asking people to give food and money. Make up posters and flyers thanking people for their donations but also advising how they can help create long-term change. For example, get people to sign a petition asking your local government to carry out research into why people are having to use food banks.

CLIMATE CHANGE

Climate change is already making it harder than ever for the world's poorest people to survive. Natural disasters and crop failures are increasingly common, creating new food emergencies all the time and causing even greater long-term food inequality.

Poorer countries often don't have the money to properly rebuild and recover after these disasters, and this can really hurt a country's development — and the lives and futures of its people.

ACTIVITY

There is a huge global youth movement against climate change, and the world is being forced to pay attention. Get inspired by young activists in countries around the world — you could ask your parents to help you find people on social media.

Read about the issues, get ideas about how you can help, and find out how you can join a local youth group against climate change. If you don't have a group locally, you could start one at your school.

CLIMATE CHANGE

Climate change is mostly caused by the lifestyles of people in the richest countries, but it is the poorest people who are often the most at risk from its effects. Extreme and unpredictable weather is already devastating communities around the world, and looks likely to become more widespread in the future.

UNEQUAL IMPACT

Extreme weather and natural disasters — such as droughts, floods, and storms — have always taken place, but they are worse now because of climate change. Many of the world's poorest people live in hotter areas, where a small rise in temperature can cause severe crop failure and push more people into poverty and hunger.

FORCED MIGRATION

Experts believe that by 2050 climate change could force 140 million people to migrate away from their homes. But this number could be cut by up to 80 percent if we take action now. Firstly, we have to stop producing gases that cause climate change. Secondly, we need to encourage investment in countries most at risk, so they can develop in ways that help them cope better with the effects of climate change.

WATER SHORTAGES

Global warming is already causing cities and regions to run dangerously low on water. It is estimated that one in nine people in the world have no access to safe drinking water, and climate change is threatening major water sources.

Many people in poorer countries spend a lot of time each day walking to collect water, and children sometimes have to help with this task instead of going to school. If the nearest sources dry up, they'll have to walk even further and spend even more time collecting water.

THINK AND ACT

At your school, organize an event where you make up news videos, social media posts, and website articles as if a climate change crisis – such as a drought or a flood – is happening in your local area. Then explain that many people are already living through these crises, and tell your audience how they can help stop climate change from pushing more people into poverty and hunger (you'll find some ideas on pages 24–25). Look into staging your event in other schools and public places, and record it!

INTENSIVE FARMING

We are dependent on the soil, and the plants that grow from it, for our food. And yet our destructive farming practices risk widespread future hunger. Food will be more expensive if it is more difficult to grow. Those in poverty, who cannot afford to pay higher prices for food, will suffer first.

SIXTY HARVESTS LEFT

Intensive farming aims to produce the maximum amount of food for the lowest price. It prioritizes short-term profits over healthy soil, stripping it of nutrients and water and not allowing it to rest and recover naturally.

Experts think that if we carry on mistreating the soil and allowing other issues such as climate change to continue damaging it, we will only have sixty harvests left before we're not able to grow any more crops at all in our planet's soil.

SOIL CRISIS

Climate change, forest destruction, and intensive farming cause many problems, including soil erosion, desertification, and salinization. Soil erosion is when the nutrient-rich top layer of soil is swept away, often by wind or water; desertification is when fertile land turns to desert; and salinization is when soil becomes too salty for most plants. These issues are creating areas around the world where little or nothing can be grown.

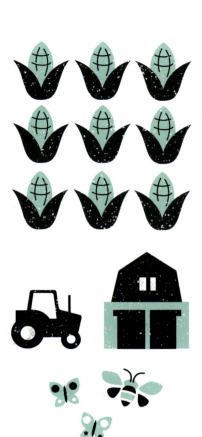

MONOCULTURES

Intensive farmers often grow monocultures – many fields of the same crop, such as wheat – rather than a mix of plants, as you would find in nature.

This means that animals can't find the right food to eat, which can eventually cause them to die. This has a domino effect throughout the food chain. It may be really bad news for farmers, too, as animals can help pollinate crops or naturally control destructive pests.

THINK AND ACT

Permaculture is a way of growing food in harmony with nature, improving the soil rather than destroying it. There are many videos online about permaculture – ask an adult to help you learn more about it.

If you have a garden or a windowsill, try out some permaculture techniques, such as creating a herb spiral. Or you could ask about planting a permaculture garden at school or in the local area, to be a real soil savior!

PESTICIDES AND HERBICIDES

We share the planet with lots of other animals, and they often want to eat our food crops! Many farmers use chemicals called pesticides to kill them off. They also use herbicides to kill weeds competing with food crops for space, water, and nutrients. More food crops for us is a good thing, right? Well ...

INSECTS

Pesticides and herbicides can poison the soil and water, killing plants and animals that don't even threaten crops. In some areas, insect populations have fallen by up to 75 percent in recent years – this is believed to be largely due to intensive farming practices (see pages 18–19). Many insects help pollinate food crops, so without them we're in big trouble.

POISONING PEOPLE

It is estimated that around 200,000 people every year die from pesticide poisoning. Others develop serious and long-term illnesses, with farmworkers – who are often low-paid – particularly at risk.

The cotton industry is one of the biggest pesticide users of all, and more people are now trying to grow cotton organically – that is, without using poisonous chemicals.

THINK AND ACT

Some high-end shops now sell clothes made with organic cotton, often in special lines with names like "Conscious" or "Eco." Do some research into whether there are any affordable clothes for young people in these lines. If there are, put them on a list you can share with others; if not, contact the company headquarters to ask them to start!

GOING ORGANIC

Growing crops organically is much better for the environment, and so in the long term should help us continue to feed the global population. But there is a risk of losing crops to disease and pests, and some people worry that on a large scale this could represent a big hunger risk.

There are many natural ways to control weeds and pests, though — for example, bringing in ladybugs to eat plant-chomping aphids. Farmers could also choose to use less destructive chemicals. Governments can, and sometimes do, ban the very worst pesticides and herbicides.

GROWING TECHNOLOGIES

Clever inventors are coming up with high-tech solutions to try to stop us going hungry despite the growing impact of climate change and unsustainable farming practices. But many are concerned they will benefit richer people and leave those in poverty to face the worst consequences of environmental destruction.

VERTICAL FARMS AND ROBOT BEES

Vertical farms grow food crops in trays of water rather than soil, and these trays are stacked up in rows to create towers. Sometimes, plants are also grown in tanks with fish in – their poop gives the plants nutrients. Scientists are also developing drones known as robot bees to pollinate plants, because populations of flying insects are continuing to fall.

ADAPT TO SURVIVE

Selective breeding can help plants and animals develop certain characteristics, including ones that make them better suited to climate change. Plants can be bred together to create varieties that may, for example, do better in hotter and drier conditions. Scientists can also change plants' genes directly, but many worry that we don't know the long-term health impact of eating these genetically modified crops.

DON'T GIVE UP

The fact that these potentially hunger-fighting technologies are available or in development shouldn't make us think we can carry on living as destructively as we do now. For a start, we still have to deal with the other impacts of climate change, such as rising sea levels.

In many parts of the world, people can't afford to set up even basic growing technology – such as irrigation systems that automatically water large areas of crops – let alone buy robot bees. We need to stand against climate change and put pressure on leaders to help poorer countries access effective, affordable growing technologies.

THINK ABOUT IT

People can be selfish and not worry about the effects of climate change and environmental issues on other people. How might you get through to someone who would rather keep doing whatever they want than help to make real change?

STAND AGAINST: FOOD DESTRUCTION

Earth provides us with enough food and water for everyone, but we are destroying its ability to do this. We can't carry on with "business as usual." If people don't stop overconsuming and start putting our planet's survival first, we will find that our home becomes an impossible place for us to live. For many, particularly the world's poorest, this is already a reality.

Start a 3 x 3 campaign to inspire as many people as possible to think and act less carelessly when it comes to the planet and our future.

STEP ONE

Come up with three things that you can do for the planet every week. It could be:

- switching off the lights whenever you leave an empty room
- eating meat only one day a week
- not buying any plastic-wrapped snacks and donating the money you save to a charity such as Friends of the Earth.

It might be helpful and fun to keep a journal about what you're doing.

STEP TWO

Ask three friends or family members to each come up with three things they can do for the planet every week. Now you're having three times the impact already – that's the power of the 3 x 3 campaign! Keep checking in with your fellow campaigners, asking them how they're doing and encouraging them to keep going.

STEP THREE

Now ask your three fellow campaigners to each sign up three more people. If these new recruits then ask three people themselves, the campaign will keep growing and growing! Ask a trusted adult to help you organize regular meetings for all the 3 x 3 campaigners, so you can support each other and plan actions together.

STEP FOUR

Now that you're all putting in this work, doesn't it feel annoying that so many companies and politicians aren't really trying to help? Contact them about starting their own 3 x 3 campaign, taking three steps every three months to work toward a more sustainable way of living and a future that's less dangerous for everyone. Keep checking up on them!

NO WAY TO WORK

Millions of people in the world are in poverty because, although they desperately want to work and support themselves, they are living in circumstances that make this incredibly difficult or even impossible.

NO JOBS

Many countries simply don't have enough jobs for everyone. This can leave lots of people unemployed or underemployed. A growing number of people feel that some charities are putting off investors by stereotyping poorer countries as backward, which makes the situation worse.

NO OPPORTUNITIES

Poverty is often most extreme in rural areas of poorer countries. Job opportunities can be very limited beyond trying to scrape together a living as a farmer with a small amount of land. Millions move to the cities each year to find work, but often there is not enough work for everyone there either.

Many people around the world — especially women — can't get a good education. They are left without the necessary skills for jobs that would lift them out of poverty. In many parts of the world, women are still expected to work full-time in the home and look after children rather than do paid work.

NO STABILITY

War, conflict, natural disasters, and public health crises — such as virus outbreaks — can disrupt countries for many years, removing all sorts of job and education opportunities. Recovery can be expensive and take a long time, leaving people without any options for work.

People may spend every penny they have trying to escape danger. They may have difficulty finding work elsewhere — often because international laws stop them from working in other countries.

THINK AND ACT

People in richer countries can be very selfish and cruel toward people escaping danger and poverty in their own countries. Write a story or create a comic about a child having to leave their home and travel to live in a new country. How do they feel? How might they want people to treat them? Share your story once it's finished.

IN-WORK POVERTY

Most people in the world who are living in poverty are actually working — it's just that their work doesn't pay them enough to cover their food, shelter, and other basic needs. This is true in both richer and poorer countries. As living costs rise but wages stay the same for many, people are pushed into poverty.

WEALTH GAP

While so many struggle in poverty, someone else is often making a lot of money from their hard work. An obvious example is that farmers and factory workers are often paid very little, but companies selling the products they've made end up making much more money.

The gap between low and high earners in society has grown enormously in recent years, with the highest-paid managers in a company often earning tens or hundreds of times more than its lowest-paid workers. Companies' profits typically go to make rich investors even richer, rather than being used to increase low wages.

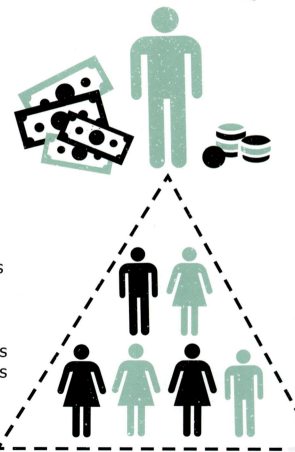

WORKERS' RIGHTS

Many people work for low wages in dangerous or unhealthy conditions, but worry they'll lose their jobs if they ask for better treatment. The law can protect workers' rights but it often serves the interests of rich employers instead. Workers can join together in groups called trade unions, and threaten to strike (stop working) if their demands for better conditions aren't met. People in power sometimes take extreme measures, including violence, to stop workers from forming trade unions.

> **THINK ABOUT IT**
>
> Some people believe that companies should only be allowed to pay their highest-earning staff a certain number of times more than their lowest-earning staff. What do you think about that idea? How many times more would be OK?

DISCRIMINATION AT WORK

Discrimination is when certain groups of people – for example, people with disabilities – are treated unfairly compared to others. They are often overlooked for better-paid roles and paid less for doing the same work. On average, black women in the U.S. earn 38 percent less than white men and 21 percent less than white women. The result is that groups who are discriminated against are more likely to face in-work poverty.

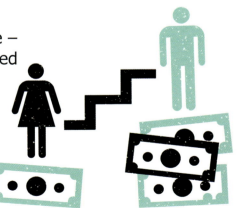

MODERN SLAVERY

Many of us think that slavery — when someone is forced to work for no pay — is a thing of the past. Sadly, that isn't the case at all. There are actually more enslaved people today than at any other time in history, and people already in poverty are particularly vulnerable to becoming victims of modern slavery.

SLAVERY TODAY

Slavery is illegal in all officially recognized countries of the world, but it is estimated that there are over 40 million enslaved people in the world today. That's more people than the entire population of Canada.

Someone living in modern slavery could be, for example: a domestic worker in a family's home; a factory worker; a child soldier; or a victim of forced child marriage. It is believed that over 70 percent of modern slaves are women.

MIGRANTS AT RISK

Many migrants trying to escape danger and poverty become trapped in modern slavery abroad, after trusting people to arrange paid work and shelter for them. Victims are forced to pay so much for very poor shelter and food that they can't ever work off their debt and get free.

Criminals also target child refugees and migrants, kidnapping them from crowds and camps and forcing them into slavery.

GETTING HELP

Victims may be too scared to try to escape because the people keeping them in slavery have threatened to hurt or kill their family. If people have been forced into illegal activity, they may also be scared of getting in trouble with the police. People who have entered the country illegally may be afraid of being sent back to their home country. Children in modern slavery often remain trapped as adults, and have no chance of an education.

THINK AND ACT

Contact three stores where your family regularly shops, and ask what they're doing to make sure no one working for them – particularly on farms and in factories – is a victim of modern slavery. If you don't think they're doing enough, boycott them – stop buying their products. You could encourage your family, friends, and neighbors to do the same, and let the store know.

STAND AGAINST:
CHILD LABOR

Child labor is still very common in some countries, affecting one in ten children in the world. It can often keep children out of school and in long-term poverty, but it can also be very dangerous. It is estimated that at least 22,000 children die at work each year, and others suffer serious health issues. As a young person, your voice speaking out for other children can be very powerful – so use it!

INDIVIDUALS

Many products are still made using child labor, and you and others could be supporting this without knowing it. People often think it's a lot of work to research everything they buy, so help out by creating a "Five Top Shopping Tips" poster with information about avoiding products made using child labor. You can share it digitally and put up paper copies.

Look on stopchildlabor.org for ideas and tell people which brands and marks (such as Fair Trade and GoodWeave) guarantee that products are child-labor free. Include a list of products that often involve child labor – such as soccer balls – and require extra-careful shopping.

COMPANIES

Go on a fact-finding mission, making a list of major stores and checking to see what they are doing to make sure no child labor is used for their products.

If you don't think the stores are doing enough, make a fuss! Companies worry about losing customers, so pressure them to act by sharing the news with as many people as possible – try a petition, video, or live event.

GOVERNMENTS

Child labor isn't illegal all over the world – different countries have different laws. If your country agrees its children should have certain rights and protections, why are children in other countries any different? Start a campaign asking your government to put pressure on other governments to change their laws, and not allow companies to sell products in your country unless they are guaranteed free from child labor.

You could ask an adult to help you stage a public event in a safe local place, with you and other children holding signs as if you were the ones doing child labor – with messages such as "I just want to go to school" and "I'm forced to breathe in dangerous chemicals as I work." Make sure the adult checks when and where you are allowed to hold this protest event.

HOUSING

Housing is often people's biggest living expense, and in lots of countries the cost of buying or renting somewhere to live has risen far quicker than wages. This has left many people unable or struggling to keep a roof over their head – in richer and poorer countries alike.

PROFITS OVER PEOPLE

While many struggle to afford basic housing, there is a rich minority of people who own multiple properties and make huge amounts of money from them. They often use their profits to buy up more property. Lots of new housing is unaffordable for anyone but the very rich, and houses sit empty because they've only been bought to sell later for more money.

UNFAIR CONDITIONS

Many people pay so much to rent housing that they can't meet other basic needs or ever save up for their own house. In many countries, renters don't have many rights and are scared of being kicked out of their homes if they complain about unsafe or unhealthy conditions.

In some countries, such as India and Brazil, millions of people live in huge slums – in houses made of cheap materials and often without electricity, running water, or a functioning sewage system.

HOMELESSNESS

It is estimated that around one hundred million people worldwide are homeless and that 1.6 billion – one in five people – don't have stable, adequate housing. As well as those living on the streets, there are many "hidden homeless" people, staying on friends' sofas and in temporary accommodations.

Homelessness is very dangerous – in the United States, homeless people die around twenty years younger than the national average. Many people worldwide are homeless because poverty, conflict, natural disasters, and the effects of climate change have forced them from their homes.

THINK AND ACT

Unaffordable housing costs push people into poverty and homelessness, so some countries have set maximum rental prices.

If your government hasn't done this yet, why not ask a trusted adult to help you record a video asking why they care more about rich adults making money than about poor and homeless children? It's a tough question for them to answer! Your trusted adult could share the video widely to get people's attention.

WELFARE SYSTEMS

Welfare systems are the ways in which a government takes care of its people when they are at the greatest risk of poverty or harm. This can include children and their parents, people who are pregnant, those who are ill or have a disability, older people, and unemployed or underpaid people.

NO SUPPORT

In many countries people don't receive much, if any, direct help from the government. This makes life very hard, and often dangerous, for people who can't support themselves and their families through work. Those who aren't able to work at all – for example, some people with serious disabilities and illnesses – may not have any money of their own, and be left in the unfair and frustrating situation of always having to rely on others.

THINK ABOUT IT

Welfare systems are largely paid for through taxes: money taken off people's and businesses' earnings. Some people don't like paying taxes and want to get rid of welfare systems altogether. Why might that make society more unequal and increase poverty levels?

NOT GOOD ENOUGH

Richer countries may have welfare systems, but even they don't always give people enough money to live on without really struggling. On top of this, in some rich countries, the government doesn't provide basic healthcare. This can mean that people have to pay huge amounts of money if they get ill or injured.

Also, people who rely on legal aid – money from the government to help them get justice, for example in the law courts – can be at an unfair disadvantage when up against richer people or companies that can afford expensive, expert legal teams.

UNFAIR WELFARE

In some countries, even those who work need welfare support because they are paid so badly and their living costs are so high. The government bridges the gap between unfairly low wages and unfairly high living expenses, using the tax money many people pay from their salaries.

This allows rich companies and landlords to go on making huge profits by underpaying and overcharging people. And although rich people should by law pay their fair share of tax to the government, some of them pay experts to find legal ways to avoid doing so.

THE POWER OF PRIVILEGE

Some people like to think that everyone has a fair chance in life now, especially in richer countries, and that the amount of money you have reflects how smart you are and how hard you have worked. That's just not the case. Society is full of systems that make it much easier for some people to succeed than others.

PRIVILEGE

Privilege is an unfair advantage given only to a certain group, and it comes in many different forms — including race, gender, and class (how rich your family is). For example, white privilege means white people are treated better as a whole in society than people of any other race.

An average person with one or more privileges is likely to have more opportunities and avoid poverty more easily than an average person without them.

EDUCATION

Education helps children get ahead in life, but it isn't free all over the world. In poorer countries, many parents can't afford to send their children to school – and girls are particularly unlikely to go.

Even free education isn't equal for all children – schools in richer areas often have more money for resources, and richer parents can afford tutoring and extracurricular activities, or even pay for private schools. This privilege has a domino effect – children from richer families are more likely to go to university and get higher-earning jobs.

INTO WORK

Young adults from richer families are more likely to receive money from their parents, allowing them to focus on their studies and do unpaid internships. But those from poorer families will probably need to do paid work to cover their living costs. Employers can help reduce this inequality by offering only paid internships.

Privileged young people are also more likely to have relatives or family friends in positions of power, who can "put in a good word" to give them an unfair advantage when applying for university spots, internships, and jobs. All this makes them much more likely to avoid poverty in the long term, and takes opportunities away from less privileged people to do the same.

THINK ABOUT IT

Do you think private schools should be allowed in countries where there is free education for all? What are the arguments for and against this?

STAYING AFLOAT

A disappointingly high number of people today still believe that people deserve to be rich or poor, that the way things are is natural and unavoidable, and that people can get by and get ahead if they just try hard enough.

In fact, unfairness is built into systems — rich, powerful, and privileged people deliberately make things work in their favor, so they get richer and everyone else stays poor. Then they blame people for not being able to cover their high living costs with their low incomes, accusing them of being lazy or wasteful.

Many people who haven't experienced poverty may not really think about how hard it is — how near impossible, or actually impossible, it is to live day to day.

ACTIVITY

Hold out your hands – or draw a pair of hands on paper. You have ten coins for the week – one per finger.

Your housing costs three coins – put down three fingers. Your basic bills and taxes cost another two coins – put two more fingers down. Food costs at least one coin, two if you want any healthy food. Transportation costs one coin, two if you need a car. So you've got one, two, or three coins left for the week. But if you want internet at home, or a mobile phone, that's another coin.

Any coins left? Ah, good, because your shoes are falling apart and you need some new shoes – that's another coin. If you'd already run out of coins, you're now on minus one.

Many people work full-time and can still barely meet their basic living costs, let alone save up or do anything fun. Does that sound fair? Meanwhile, a big boss working at their company might earn a thousand coins a week. With that much to spare, of course they would think it's easy to get by!

The activity above doesn't even factor in other common, unavoidable expenses. What if you have children or older relatives to care for, or have to pay for healthcare? You'll get further and further into debt every week.

STAND AGAINST: CHILD POVERTY

Nearly 385 million children today live in extreme poverty, lacking basic essentials such as safe drinking water, food, shelter, and healthcare. This issue is particularly severe in certain areas – for example, half of all children in sub-Saharan Africa are growing up in extreme poverty. So, what can you do to help solve this problem for good?

SEE THE FUTURE

Child poverty kills thousands of children every day, and those who survive into adulthood often suffer domino effects that may continue for the rest of their lives. For example, a lack of nutritious food, clean water, and reliable healthcare can cause serious long-term health and development issues that should be preventable today.

Create an infographic – an imaginative visual way to present data – to show how children are affected by poverty, and what needs to be done to fix it. Aim to help people see the current emergency, but also its long-term negative effects and how it will keep hurting people in the future.

EDUCATE THE FUTURE

Education is the best way to break the cycle of poverty, in which children from poorer families are more likely to experience poverty as adults. A good education helps children learn skills that open up more opportunities to move out of poverty.

Hold an event raising money for education charities and groups that campaign for a good, free education for every child in the world. Come up with a catchy slogan that captures the idea of children wanting to be in control of their own futures – such as "Help us to not need your help!"

CHANGE THE FUTURE

In the future, more and more children may be pushed into poverty by the effects of climate change. Adults will be affected too, of course, but children are likely to outlive them and may therefore face increasingly dire conditions.

Create a video called "Things Can't Only Get Better," focusing on how we can prevent climate change having an even worse impact on children's futures. For example, we could reduce how much meat we eat, or support aid for poorer countries to cope with extreme weather.

BE THE CHANGE, SPREAD THE WORD

>> You are connected to so many people — in your family, your neighborhood, at school, online, and maybe in after-school groups and at your religious or cultural center. By taking action yourself, and showing others how and why they should get involved too, you can make a real difference to people experiencing poverty and hunger.

HUMAN RIGHTS

The Universal Declaration of Human Rights is a document that lays out all the rights that every human should have — including the right to freedom, education, healthcare, food, safe housing, safe work, and leisure time (play time for children). You can find a copy of it online. Hold a human rights event at school, using this document to explore different types of inequality.

Students could research how a particular human right can be put at risk or violated by poverty and hunger. For example, someone living in poverty might not be able to afford safe housing. Students could put on presentations, or create videos or short plays, to share what they've learned and explain how people can help create positive change.

FOOD WASTE

One third of all food produced is wasted. You might think, "It's not as if that food would otherwise have gone to someone hungry, though." But the more food we waste, the bigger impact we're having on the planet, and for no reason. We are using too many natural resources as it is, but all this extra waste makes the problem even worse.

Try having a zero-waste goal in your home for a week, where you make sure to eat all the food you have in the house and not let any of it go bad. If any food does get wasted, write it up on a board where everyone in your house will see it. Every week, try to beat last week's record for as little waste as possible.

Why not try out this zero-waste challenge in your school cafeteria, too? Ask your teachers and classmates to help you organize it.

THINK AND ACT

Can you think of some other creative ways to inspire more people to help stand against **poverty and hunger?**

Glossary

climate change – changes in weather patterns and temperatures around the world, caused by human activity

debt – money that someone has borrowed and has to pay back to a person or organization

discrimination – when someone receives unfairly negative treatment because they are part of a certain group

food bank – a place where people who can't afford to buy enough food can get basic supplies for free

fossil fuel – a fuel such as oil or coal that was formed over millions of years from the remains of plants and animals

herbicide – a chemical used to kill unwanted plants

indigenous people – groups of people whose ancestors originally lived in an area before others arrived

inequality – the unfair situation of some people having a lot and others having very little

irrigation – a system of giving plants water without people watering them by hand

malnutrition – when somebody isn't getting enough nutrients (vitamins and other things that a body needs to stay healthy) from their food

migrant – someone who moves from where they usually live to another place, often to try to find better living conditions or opportunities

organic – a product that is grown or made without using pesticides and other chemicals

overconsumption – buying and using far more than is necessary

pesticide – a chemical used to kill unwanted creatures

private school – a school that is funded by people paying money for their children to attend, rather than receiving money from the government

privilege – when someone receives unfairly positive treatment because they are part of a certain group

slum – a crowded, poorly built area of a town or city where living conditions are typically very bad

stereotype – a set idea that people have about what someone or something is like

subsidize – when the government pays money to make certain products cheaper for people to buy

trade union – a group of workers who join together to ask for better pay and conditions

underemployed – not having enough paid work, or having to do work that doesn't make proper use of your skills and knowledge

Further information

BOOKS

Poverty (Our World in Crisis)
Rachel Minay (Franklin Watts, 2018)
This book looks at the causes of poverty and how it affects people all over the world. It investigates what action is currently being taken to tackle poverty, and how you might be able to help.

The Crops We Grow (Eco STEAM)
Georgia Amson-Bradshaw (Wayland, 2018)
Learn more about the challenges of farming and growing crops, and how we can feed the world without causing so much damage to our planet. Take on interactive challenges and complete step-by-step activities to practice putting your ideas and knowledge into action.

WEBSITES

www.lovefoodhatewaste.com/
Learn more about why it's important to save food, how you can best store and reuse food, and how it all adds up. Review this website with a trusted adult and come up with a plan to produce less food waste.

medium.com/@hccb/how-kids-can-help-homeless-8adca96a87dc
Ask a trusted adult to look through this website with you as you discover how you can help people who are experiencing homelessness.

Note to parents and teachers: every effort has been made by the Publishers to ensure websites are suitable for children, that they are of the highest educational value, and that they contain no inappropriate or offensive material. However, because of the nature of the internet, it is impossible to guarantee that the contents of these sites will not be altered. We strongly advise that internet access is supervised by a responsible adult.

Index

biofuel 9

charities 11, 24, 26, 43
children 5, 12, 13, 17, 26, 27, 30, 31, 32–33, 35, 36, 39, 41, 42–43, 44
climate change 7, 9, 10, 15, 16–17, 18, 22, 23, 35, 43

debt 6, 30, 41
disabilities 13, 29, 36
discrimination 29

education 26, 27, 31, 39, 43, 44

farming 8, 10, 18–19, 20, 21, 22, 26, 28, 31
food 8–9, 10–11, 12–13, 14–15, 18, 19, 20, 22, 24, 28, 30, 41, 42, 44, 45

health 4, 11, 12, 13, 20, 22, 27, 29, 32, 34, 37, 41, 42, 44
herbicides 20
housing 34–35, 41, 44
human rights 44

indigenous people 8
inequality 5, 11, 14–15, 39, 44
infographic 42

land 8, 9, 12, 18, 26
laws 27, 29, 33, 37
living costs 37, 39, 40, 41

meat 8, 9, 13, 24, 43
migration 16, 30
modern slavery 30–31
monocultures 19

natural disasters 10, 15, 16, 27, 35
nutrition 12, 13, 14

organic 20, 21

permaculture 19
pesticides 20
petition 13, 14, 33
privilege 38–39, 40

shopping 6, 7, 13, 32
soil 18, 19, 20, 22

technology 22–23
transportation 7, 10, 11, 41

veganism 9
vegetarianism 8, 9

war 10, 27
waste 7, 45
water 4, 17, 18, 20, 22, 23, 24, 34, 42
welfare 36–37
women 26, 29, 30
work 13, 20, 26, 27, 28–29, 30, 31, 32, 33, 36, 37, 38, 39, 41, 44